T0077817

IN SEARCH
OF THE
LOST SHEEP

IN SEARCH OF THE LOST SHEEP

"FOR THE SON OF MAN HAS COME TO SEEK
AND TO SAVE THAT WHICH WAS LOST."
LUKE 19:10

Calet Cortes Jr.
&
Marisol Bennett

IN SEARCH OF THE LOST SHEEP

"For the Son of Man has come to seek and to save that which was lost." Luke 19:10

iUniverse books may be ordered through booksellers or by contacting:

Scripture quotations marked KJV are from the Holy Bible, King James Version (Authorized Version). First published in 1611. Quoted from the KJV Classic Reference Bible, Copyright © 1983 by The Zondervan Corporation.

iUniverse
1663 Liberty Drive
Bloomington, IN 47403
www.iuniverse.com
1-800-Authors (1-800-288-4677)

ISBN: 978-1-4917-0323-6 (sc)
ISBN: 978-1-4917-0324-3 (e)

Print information available on the last page.

iUniverse rev. date: 05/12/2015

Contents

PREFACE

The passion upon writing this book came about after realizing that not only am I limited to reaching the lost by means of preaching, teaching, giving to the needy or performing plays and dramas; but that I can write down everything I have experienced, good and bad and proclaim the good news of salvation as the people read.

This book is written to bring inspiration, hope and peace to those seeking more in life. I am in search of the lost sheep and this is why my decision to write this book is so important to me.

"What is the lost sheep?" You might ask; well if a shepherd has 100 sheep and one of them goes astray, don't you think that shepherd will go out of his way to find that lost sheep? "Yes," he would. And when that lost sheep is found, the shepherd rejoices because he found the one that was lost and now is safe in his arms. It is now time for me to introduce to you the one you can run to and the one who can keep you safe in his arms.

As you read this book, I pray that you will understand that there is a Shepherd who will take you in His arms and turn your life around to start a fresh new beginning where you will find peace, hope, love and joy everlasting. Jesus is our Shepherd and we are the sheep. As it is written in the bible, John 10:11 says, "I am the good shepherd: the good shepherd giveth his life for the sheep."

DEDICATION OF THIS BOOK

To my loving and supportive wife Alicia, without whose support this book would have never happened. She is a loving partner, gentle mother, virtuous woman but most of all, a true prayer warrior.

To my father Calet Cortes Senior and my mother Miriam Cortes who are always faithful in their prayers.

To my son Edward and his wife Sandra Cortes. To my daughter Elizabeth who has always been by my side assisting the ministry with her useful hands and gifted ideas. She knows how to create an atmosphere of fun and excitement for the young and old.

To my daughter Marisol who supported and assisted me in writing this book. To my son-in-law Recardo Bennett who has always encouraged me and continues to pray for this ministry.

To my Grandchildren Daniel, Richie, Lillian, Jason, Michael, Brianna and Sophia who are always in my heart, in my prayers and know that one day will read this book and be blessed by it.

ACKNOWLEDGEMENTS

I want to give thanks to **Mr. Clint P. Owens,** Director of Here's Life Inner City-New York City, and **Mr. Jim Bites** for providing us with lots of boxes of Easter bags to give to the Children of the Community and also for providing lots of boxes of frozen Tyson chicken every year. We were able to give to the homeless and also to give to the Community. Thank you for providing us with banana boxes filled with lots of canned goods. As a result of us giving these love boxes, people have re-dedicated their lives to Christ and that is a victory. We are so appreciative for all that you have done for this ministry.

I would like to express my appreciation to my brother-in-law **Rev. Efrain Rodriguez Sr**. of Final Quest Outreach Ministries. Please accept my heartfelt thanks for your gift donations to our ministry. If you ever need me to help with a charitable cause of your own, please let me return the favor. Thank you.

I want to express my appreciation to Brother **Douglass Velasquez** for his generosity and support to this ministry. Your personal commitment was incredibly helpful and allowed us to reach our goal. Your assistance means so much to me, but even more to: "In Search of the Lost Sheep Ministries." Thank you.

I wish to thank **Rev. Weiner Antonsanti** and the members of his church for their collaboration with this ministry. Generosity is a sign of a great soul. Thank you for everything Rev. Weiner and thank you to all the members for their love, faithfulness, prayers, support and contributions.

I would like to give my appreciation to **Pastor Irene Wallace** of Friendly Christian Church located in Brooklyn, New York for her love service to our ministry. She would always donate boxes of food so that we can give to the community. It was always a great blessing to all.

I am really grateful for my grand-daughter **Lillian Torres**. Lillian is a very ambitious young lady who is always eager to serve in the house of the Lord. She would help the ministry by creating flyers, banners and even videos for us while I was Pastor of *The Second Evangelical Crusade* church. I am very grateful for all the work that she has done for us throughout the years. May God bless you Lilly.

We greatly appreciate Reverend **Anthony Miranda** from Elohim Christian Church located in Richmond Hill, New York. Thank you for liberally contributing your time to assemble and organize canned foods and clothes to the community. By the help of your donations, gifts and contributions, we were able to feed many homeless and needy people. May God bless you always.

I want to express my appreciation to my sister **Elizabeth Rodriguez** for helping us in our ministry. Elizabeth is a great blessing to us, as she is constantly helping our ministry with her clerical support. Thank you for all you've done for this ministry.

I want to thank **Pastor Javier Dextre** for all the work he did while I was the Pastor of *The Second Evangelical Crusade* church. I am very grateful for your kindness and for contributing your time to this ministry. Thank you very much.

I am so grateful to Rev. **Sonia Bonano**. There are no words to express my gratitude for all you've done. Thank you so much for your love offerings. I will always be grateful to you and your congregation for the thoughtfulness and consideration you have given us. Thank you from the bottom of my heart.

I want to give a special thanks to Sister **Evarista De Jesus**, Sister **Carolina Velasquez**, Sister **Vatalina Gomez**, Sister and Brother **Milagros and Rogelio Valera,** my biological sisters **Maria Ripoll** and **Margie Cortes, Arlene** and her husband **Jose Garcia, Evelyn** and her husband **Joshua Echeverria**; My cousins **Maria** and **Pablo Diaz**; Sister **Elba Quintero**, Brother **Rene Cabrera**, Brother **Fausto Cabrera**, Brother **Nelson Ramos** and Brother **Cain Narvaez, Eloi,** Brother **Adrian**, Brother **Emiliano Natal**, **Antonio Venegas** and Brother **William Merino**. I want to thank all those who worked in the church while under my pastoral care.

I would like to thank Bishop **Nelson L. Aponte**, my Senior Pastor for being the person that God used for my ordination to work as Lead Pastor of "The Second Evangelical Crusade" church. I am so grateful that you heard God's voice and thank you for all that you have done for me.

INTRODUCTION

As human beings, we make our own decisions and we tend to set our own ways and direction in life; but not all ways may be the right choice or the wise decision. Many times we can be stubborn and self-centered believing that the way we think is right is the one that will lead us to blessings, prosperity, love, peace and happiness when in fact it can be the contrary.

The Bible talks about a man who had two sons. One of them made a decision that led to him being "lost" in a world where no one would care for his needs. He was what I consider a "lost sheep" because he needed the loving arms of his father who would accept him, forgive him and have compassion over him. As you read the passage on "The Parable of the Lost Son" which is found in Luke 15:11-32, remember that there is a Shepherd who always has his arms wide open to receive you and you are very valuable to Him.

THE PARABLE OF THE LOST SON

The message of the Prodigal son is a message of redemption and forgiveness. The Parable of the Prodigal son is a good message for every person whether they are believers or unbelievers because it shows the mercy of God and how willing he is to forgive all who come to him in repentance. Psalms 103:10-14 says, [10] He hath not dealt with us after our sins; nor rewarded us according to our iniquities. (He does not treat us as our sins deserve). [11] For as the heaven is high above the earth, so great is his mercy toward them that fear him. [12] As far as the east is from the west, so far hath he removed our transgressions from us. [13] Like as a father pitieth his children, so the Lord pitieth them that fear him. [14] For he knoweth our frame; he remembers that we are dust.

Romans 10:9-10 says, [9] "That if thou shalt confess with thy mouth the Lord Jesus, and shalt believe in thine heart that God hath raised him from the dead, thou shalt be saved. [10] For with the heart man believeth unto righteousness; and with the mouth confession is made unto salvation.

Please use your imagination and open your heart as you read the following passages about the prodigal son. Whether it portrays your life or someone else's life, here you can see how great our father's love is for his children and how much we mean to him.

Luke 15:11-32: says: [11] And he said, A certain man had two sons: [12] And the younger of them said to his father, Father, give me the portion of goods that falleth to me. And he divided unto them his living. [13] And not many days after the younger son gathered all together, and took his journey into a far country, and there wasted his substance with riotous living. [14] And when he had spent all, there arose a mighty famine in that land; and he began to be in want. [15] And he went and joined himself to a citizen of that country; and he sent him into his fields to feed swine. [16] He longed to fill his stomach with the pods that the pigs were eating, but no one gave him anything.[17] And when he came to himself, he said, How many hired servants of my father's have bread enough and to spare, and I perish with hunger! [18] I will arise and go to my father, and will say unto him, Father, I have sinned against heaven, and before thee, [19] And am no more worthy to be called thy son: make me as one of thy hired servants. [20] And he arose, and came to his father. But when he was yet a great way off, his father saw him, and had compassion, and ran, and fell on his feet, and kissed him. [21] And the son said unto him, Father, I have sinned against heaven, and in thy sight, and am no more worthy to be called thy son. [22] But the father said to his servants, Bring forth the best robe, and put it on him; and put a ring on his hand, and shoes on his feet: [23] And bring hither the fatted calf, and kill it; and let us eat, and be merry: [24] For this my son was dead, and is alive again; he was lost, and is found. And they began to be merry. [25] Now his elder son was in the field: and as he came and drew near to the house, he heard music and dancing. [26] And he called one of the servants, and asked what these things meant. [27] And he said unto him, Thy brother is come; and thy father hath killed the fatted calf, because he hath received him safe and sound. [28] And he was angry, and would not go in: therefore came his father out, and intreated him. [29]But he answered his father, 'Look! All these years I've been slaving for you and never disobeyed your orders. Yet you never gave me even a young goat so I could celebrate with my friends. [30] But when this son of yours who has squandered your property with prostitutes comes home, you kill the fattened calf for him! [31] And he said unto him, Son, thou art ever with me, and all that I have is yours. [32] But we had to celebrate and be glad, because this brother of yours was dead and is alive again; he was lost and is found.'" In the same way, God actively seeks those of us who have strayed in our walk of Faith as well as those who do not have a personal relationship with him. As in the story of "The Lost Sheep" in which you are going to read more about, no matter how much you've messed up, no matter what your background is, no matter how bad you've been and no matter how unworthy you may feel, Jesus, The Good Shepherd will bring you home and make you feel like you are worth more than gold and silver because He cares for you and He wants you to come to His loving arms.

CHAPTER 1

HOPE IN CHRIST

I would like to reiterate on Adam and Eve who were the first people God created on earth. Adam and Eve lived in a beautiful garden that God had created for their pleasure. They had a perfect relationship with God. They walked and talked with God and everything they had was supposed to be ours.

Because of Adam's decision which eventually led to sin, he passed on to all mankind a sinful nature. Adam and Eve gave into temptation and disobeyed God. Shame and guilt entered their lives and created a barrier between them and God. The consequences of their disobedience and lack of self-control unfortunately are with us until this day.

Today, we can see all kinds of physical illnesses and emotional issues and sufferings that have erupted as a result of Adam and Eve's disobedience to God. This is why we can see that instead of blessing there is cursing, instead of liberty there is captivity, instead of prosperity there is poverty and sickness instead of health.

I can list a whole host of other things such as; fear, loneliness, anger, depression, suicidal thoughts, addictions, death, abortions, war, child abuse, homosexuality, and so many other detestable things that have taken the place of the heavenly perfection that was destroyed because of sin; but I have good news. You can choose to accept these things or you can choose to run to the one who can make all things new for you.

Despite all of these things, "Do you think there is hope for mankind? Is there any way to escape this sinful condition that man inherited from Adam? Well praise God! There is. The Bible says in Romans 3:23 $^{23"}$ For all have sinned, and come short of the glory of God; Now I see why I was in the condition that I was in. I was separated from God and I needed to repent.

I am so happy to say that the truth has transformed my life. Jesus took our sins away and nailed them to a cross. In Jesus Christ, everything that Adam lost is restored to us. If we are in Christ, we no longer have to be in the condition that we were in.

The Bible says in 2 Corinthians 5:17, [17] "Therefore if any man be in Christ, he is a new creature: old things are passed away; behold, all things are become new." Also, in John 3:7, it states, [7] "Marvel not that I said unto thee, Ye must be born again." To be born again simply means to turn away from sin and follow Jesus. When this happens, the Spirit of God transforms your life and you have a new life in Christ.

I felt forgiveness in my heart when I let Jesus Christ come in. In doing so, he put in me the conviction of telling others about Jesus and His salvation and about the peace that we can have through Him. This reminded me when Jesus chose Ananias, one of His disciples; to tell Paul (before he became a Believer) [15] "Go! This man is my chosen instrument to proclaim my name to the Gentiles and their kings and to the people of Israel". He chose Paul to be the one to tell the people that there is a God who saves and who forgives and has the power to change your life from darkness to light.

Today, we are on the same mission in which Matthew 24:14 mentions, [14] "And this gospel of the kingdom shall be preached in all the world for a witness unto all nations; and then shall the end come. The Bible says in Isaiah 61: 1-3; "The Spirit of the Sovereign Lord is on me, because the Lord has appointed me to proclaim good news to the poor. He has sent me to bind up the brokenhearted, to proclaim freedom for the captives and release from darkness the prisoners, [2] to proclaim the year of the Lord's favor and the day of vengeance of our God, to comfort all who mourn, [3]and provide for those who grieve in Zion; to bestow on them a crown of beauty instead of ashes, the oil of joy instead of mourning, and a garment of praise instead of a spirit of despair."

This is the mission that I have chosen to lead because I know that through this, many lives can be changed and begin to see freedom, to find peace and be assured that they are not alone and don't need to be in despair. This is good news that everyone should want to hear and accept because it is life and it is hope.

We need to be like the Samaritan woman the Bible talks about in John 4: 28, 29, and 30. She stopped what she was doing just so that she can spread the word about the man she believed was the Messiah. At first, the woman had a bad reputation of being unclean and a sinner. She was rejected by other women for her immorality. As a result, she was not happy with herself. She had a void inside that she was not able to fill with everything she tried; but after having an encounter with Jesus by the well, the woman left her water jar beside the well and went back to the village and told everyone, [29] "come, see a man who told me everything I ever did. Could this be the Messiah? [30] "They came out of the town and made their way toward him." You see, Jesus showed that his mission was for the entire earth, not just the Jew. Our human tendency is to judge others, but Jesus treats people as individuals, accepting them with love and compassion. What comfort and relief must the Samaritan woman have felt knowing that her life was messed up and feeling a sense of unworthiness, yet she felt accepted and knew she was forgiven when she let Jesus walk into her life.

I just want to point out that very few people that came to Jesus didn't come to seek truth. They came to get relief, none the less, when Jesus would satisfy their needs by healing their leprosy, blindness or paralyzed bodies, once their needs were met, they were eager to know the truth about the man who helped them with their problem that could not be solved by any other means.

Most believers are looking for relief, not just the truth. Here is an example of what I am talking about. The Bible talks about "a woman who had a flow of blood for twelve years." She had spent a great deal of time trying to find the one doctor she could find for her condition. She had spent all the money she had, yet instead of getting better she grew worse. "When she heard about Jesus," just as I am letting you know about him today, she came up behind Him in the crowd and touched his garment because she thought that if she just touched his clothes she would be healed. When she did this, immediately her bleeding stopped and she felt in her body that she had received her healing. Today you don't have to touch his garment; all you need to do is;

1. *Admit that you are a sinner,*
2. *Repent and turn from your sin.*
3. *Believe that Jesus Christ died for you on the Cross and*
4. *Receive Him through prayer into your heart.*

CHAPTER 2

CONSEQUENCE OF SIN

In Chapter 3 of the book of Jonah, we read that God called Jonah to warn the people of Nineveh. He told them that they would face destruction if they refused to repent of their sins, but Jonah would rather have died than to obey God's command. Jonah wanted God to destroy the wicked Assyrian capital. He didn't want the people to repent and to receive God's forgiveness. So Jonah boarded a ship and headed in the opposite direction. What came after that was simply because of the choice Jonah had made which was the choice of being disobedient to God's voice. The life of every person on the ship was threatened by the great storm as well because of Jonah's disobedience.

The sailors sought the guilty party. Jonah quickly suggested that he be thrown overboard just as if he wanted to die. It seems he preferred death instead of taking the good news to the Godless Ninevites which God had intended for him to do. God had put Jonah in the belly of the great fish for three days to get Jonah's attention. In the end, Jonah finally admitted that he was helpless and asked God for deliverance. God set him free then Jonah reluctantly headed to Nineveh to warn the people of their punishment.

We can see here with the story of Jonah that although he had refused to obey God, God never gave up on him. God had to use a great storm and a great fish to teach Jonah about compassion and forgiveness. He could have avoided the storm and could have avoided being in the belly of a great fish if he had just obeyed from the very beginning.

God loves you so much that he would have another person go through some storms to come and reach out to you because he loves you and he doesn't want you to be lost. God chose Jonah to go to Nineveh in search of the lost sheep. He wanted Jonah to express how much God loves the people of Nineveh; how much mercy he has on them and how much compassion he has for people.

After all, God desires to bring Salvation to all humanity. John 3:16 says that "For God so loved the world that he gave his one and only son, that whoever believes in him shall not perish but have eternal life." We can see how God from day one has been on a mission, and that is to be in search of the lost sheep. He called Adam and said "Adam, where are you?" and today he is still asking that same question to many of you. He knows where you are but he wants you to come to him on your own free will just like in the story of the lost son who came back on his own free will. He wants to give you forgiveness and salvation.

There are many benefits for obeying God. When we obey God he protects us because we trust him and we are his sheep. An example of this would be the story of Daniel which you can find in the book of Daniel Chapter 6. Daniel trusted God so much that he didn't care what the people said they would do to him for praying to his God. The more he knew of what the people planned to do to him because of his faith, the more he prayed. Daniel 6:10 says ". . . . three times a day he got down on his knees and prayed, giving thanks to his God, just as he had done before." When Daniel was cast into the lion's den, God sent an angel to shut the beasts' mouths. He came out safe and untouched by the lions because he trusted in his God and he knew that God was his Great Shepherd.

When you obey God he delivers you from things you would not even imagine. Another story we can see in regards to obedience is the story of Shadrach, Meshach and Abednego who were Jews who refused to serve and worship the image of gold that king Nebuchadnezzar had set up. We read in the book of Daniel in Chapter 3 that whoever didn't bow down and worshipped this image were thrown into a fiery furnace. Being aware of this, the three men still trusted in their God whom they knew was alive and ready to rescue them.

Shadrach, Meshach and Abednego made their choice of not worshipping the golden image so they were tied up and thrown into the fiery furnace. To king Nebuchadnezzar's surprise, he didn't see only the three men in the furnace but he said "Look! I see four men walking around in the fire, unbound and unharmed, and the fourth looks like a son of gods" Daniel 3:25. When the three men came out of the furnace, their bodies were not harmed, nothing on them was burned and they didn't even smell like smoke! It was not only proof to the king that their God was real but it shows how God can and will rescue us from danger and situations in our lives when we trust and obey him.

There are always consequences for the choices and decisions we make in life. But if we choose to listen and obey, good things will come in ways you never thought of. We are able to conquer temptations and we can discipline ourselves and cover ourselves with self-control in order to avoid the consequence of sin but we can only do that with the help of Jesus. Romans 8:37 says "In all these things we are more than conquerors though him who loved us." We can come to Him and he will give us the strength to do what's right and to obey His Word so that our lives can be pleasing to Him.

Living for God is not all a bed of roses. It is difficult to do right when all you see around you are problems, pain, sorrow, sickness and discouragement but if we put our trust in God, we can defeat these occurrences in our lives and if we add prayer to that we can conquer it all. Giving in to sin will always lead to us feeling anguished, depressed and many times resulting in death; for the Bible says "For the **wages of sin** *is* death, but the gift **of** God *is* eternal life in Christ Jesus our Lord." Romans 6:23.

Praying can really make a difference in our choices and decisions. Prayer as we know is just simply talking to God. The bible says in Matthew 6:8 "Do not be like them, for your Father knows what you need before you ask him." God knows our needs, desires, hopes and dreams but he likes when we come to him and talk to him about how we feel, what we want and our desires. He longs to hear from us his children.

When we pray God releases the answers to our prayers faster than when we do not pray. Giving our weaknesses to him and asking him to help us through things in life that are difficult to bear is a start to living a free life in Christ because we are giving him our failures, our sorrows, our pain, our hopes, and we are placing it under *his control*. He then gives us the strength and the power to overcome those things which causes us to sin.

When our loved ones are going through hardships in their lives such as with addictions, depression, incurable diseases, marital issues, etc. we feel hurt and so we take it to the Lord in prayer, just like God would want us to do. We should reward our problems, pain, debt, sorrow, discouragement, sickness and fear with prayer and God will give us the strength just as he gave David who killed Goliath with a slingshot and stones, to overcome.

We can destroy all of these attacks with prayer and by putting our trust in God who helps us triumph. Romans 8:38-39 says "Now in all these things we are more than conquerors through him who loved us. [38] For I am convinced that neither death nor life, neither angels nor demons, neither the present nor the future, nor any powers, [39] neither height nor depth, nor anything else in all creation, will be able to separate us from the love of God that is in Christ Jesus our Lord.

Prayer has a place of highest priority in the bible. Many of the people we read about in the bible who have committed murder, have lied and cheated, have cried out to God in prayer because they knew that he was the only way, the only solution and the only way out. There will be times in which you will not know how to pray or what to say but God knows this about us because Romans 8:26 states that "In the same way, the Spirit helps us in our weakness. We do not know what we ought to pray for, but the Spirit himself intercedes for us through wordless groans."

When you pray, it is not important how long you pray for or what type of words you use. Just as how you may talk to your spouse or a friend you can talk to God because he knows your heart and he knows the sincerity of your heart. Matthew 6:7 says "And when you pray, do not keep on babbling like pagans, for they think they will be heard because of their many words. When you pray you don't have to be focused on the many words or the duration of time. What is important is that you make it a priority and make it a time to be alone with God to give him all the praise and thanksgiving as well as all of your cares, worries and requests. Philippians 4:6 says, "Do not be anxious about anything, but in every situation, by prayer and petition, with thanksgiving, present your requests to God."

Perhaps you think that prayer is something that might not work for you, well Matthew 15:18 says, "But the things that come out of a person's mouth come from the heart, and these defile them." If you don't believe that prayer will help you get through your situations and help you to avoid the consequences of sin, then that is what is in your heart and you might just pass up on many answered prayers if you had just trusted in the one who can keep you from harm's way.

Perhaps this might encourage you to pray today and to wait for your prayers to be answered. Below are some of the people who received answers to their prayers in the bible:

Exodus 33:12-23:
Moses prayed for God's presence and God's glory came down.

Joshua 7:6-26:
God answered Joshua's prayer of despair.

Samuel 1:1-28:
Hannah prayed and God answered.

1Kings 18:41-46 and James 5:17-18:
Elijah prayed and God answered.

2Kings 19:14-37:
Hezekiah prayed and God answered.

Ephesians 1:15-23
Paul prayed for knowledge and wisdom and God answered.

There are so many more that I can mention but as we can see, we cannot give up on seeking God's face and talking to him because he is all, knows all and is our best advocate.

We can come to him freely and he will lift us up because we are his children, we are his sheep which he will never forsake and let go. He wants the best for all of us and will always be there to hear our every prayer.

CHAPTER 3

LIKE IN THE DAYS OF NOAH

(Repentance)

Matthew 24: 37 says, "As it was in the days of Noah, so it will be at the coming of the Son of Man." "People were eating, drinking, marrying and being given in marriage up to the day Noah entered the ark. Then the flood came and destroyed them all." Luke 17:27. The people in the days of Noah were very wicked as we can see by reading the book of Genesis. Genesis 6:11-12 says "Now the earth was corrupt in God's sight and was full of violence. ¹² God saw how corrupt the earth had become, for all the people on earth had corrupted their ways.

God was very disappointed by his creation, how the hearts of the people were enticed just to do evil. God was sorry that he made man on earth and he grieved in his heart. He still wanted to give them a chance to repent and that is why he let Noah preach one hundred and twenty years before sending his judgment. God knew that all of these people represented the lost sheep and he wanted to save them from destruction. The people refused to enter the ark that Noah had made by the instructions of God. The consequence of their disobedience ultimately brought death to all of them.

In today's world, we are seeing many of the same things that were seen in Noah's time. Today people have no time for God. They are too busy eating, drinking, marrying, and having fun. Everything else to them is not important or of any relevance. It is good to have fun when there is no sin involved but when you leave God out of the picture, things will start to crumble and eventually lead to destruction.

The difference we have today is that we have the advantage of hearing the gospel of Jesus Christ through various means and not through just one man. One man was enough to reach the people that were called to enter the ark but they refused to listen. Now we have millions of Bibles we can read in all languages. We have television broadcasts with all different kinds of teachings and preaching's. We have churches on almost every street corner. There is no excuse not to enter Noah's Ark. It is a safe haven. Once you enter in, your life becomes new.

When you turn away from sin, it is called "repentance." When you repent, you feel remorseful about the sin you committed and deep in your heart you feel guilty about what you've done. It's when you really know and realize that what you did was wrong and hurtful to God. When you repent, you choose not to go back to those things that you knew were wrong and you make a decision to live your life pleasing to God.

This change of mind may not be an easy thing to do because you may be used to living in sin and have gotten comfortable with the lifestyle you have lived in but because of your faith and because of your obedience, repentance not only can become effortless, but the holy spirit will give you the strength to move forward. At that point, you will begin to develop a new mind, new heart and new life. 2 Corinthians 5:17 says, "[17] Therefore, if anyone is in Christ, he is a new creation. The old has gone, the new has come." Once we repent, all of our sins are forgiven and never remembered by God. Psalms 103: 11-12 says, "For as high as the heavens are above the earth, so great is his love for those who fear him;[12] as far as the east is from the west, so far has he removed our transgressions from us. Wouldn't that make you feel great? To know that you can come to him, repent, and none of your sins are remembered? That comes only with true repentance from the heart.

Jesus is knocking at the door of your heart and he is asking you to let him in so that he can give you peace and salvation. Jesus is the Ark. Jesus said, "I am the door, if anyone enters by me, he will be saved." John 10:9. Jesus says, "Here I am! I stand at the door and knock. If anyone hears my voice and opens the door, I will come in and eat with that person, and they with me." Revelation 3:20. The door of mercy will soon be closed to the wicked, just like the door of Noah's Ark was closed and no one could come in. Today is the day of salvation. Why won't you let Jesus into your heart so you too can be saved?

CHAPTER 4

MY TESTIMONY

I, Calet, was born in Ponce, Puerto Rico. I came to New York City in 1957 where unfortunately the circumstances of my life led me to substance abuse. In this case, the substance abuse was alcohol. For years I struggled with alcohol. I failed to finish high school. Although I always worked, my illness remained with me. When I met Alicia who is now my wife, I still drank alcohol with a passion and never stopped. I wanted to stop but was unable to.

Then an opportunity came to me that changed everything. There was a person out there who was in search of the lost sheep and that lost sheep was me. I didn't feel good about myself. I had lost hope. I had anger, anxiety and was very worried about what was going to happen to me if I had kept drinking. This person looked me in the eye and said: "Young man, God is able to set you free from that addiction of alcohol", and I answered him and asked, "How is that?" This man whom I realized afterwards was just a servant of God, said: "The bible says that you will know the truth and the truth will set you free."

He began to explain to me God's plan of Salvation for my life. He mentioned that when God's son Jesus, died on the Cross, he took the punishment for my sin which I deserved. He said that through his death we have been forgiven: John 3:16 says, "For God so loved the world that he gave his only son, that whoever believes in him will not perish but have eternal life." So I did believe him. That night there was a prayer service in my father's house and there was a young lady by the name of Aida Guzman who asked my wife and I if we wanted to accept Jesus into our heart and we said yes. Ever since that day God has changed our lives. We became members of a church by the name of *La Cruzada Evangelica* where the pastors there were Reverend Ismael and Flora Colon. There my wife Alicia sang hymns and songs for the glory of God as I performed with dramatizations for the purpose of seeking the lost.

My ministry in the church began with being a servant which I still am but I began by cleaning the sanctuary and making sure everything was ready for the next service to be held. I then began the drama ministry which included Christmas productions, Resurrection Sunday productions and even did some specials for the mother's on Mother's Day and for the fathers on Father's Day. This is how I started out, doing it all to reach the lost sheep and that's where I came up with the "In Search of the Lost Sheep" play where the story of "The Lost Sheep" was acted out and my passion developed from there on.

I, along with my wife had the opportunity to travel to Puerto Rico and was able to perform the play "In Search of the Lost Sheep" in various churches in which many people got saved through. Many years later a new pastor took over *La Cruzada Evangelica* by the name of Reverend Nelson Aponte in which I was also given the privilege to travel with to different countries such as Mexico and Spain sharing the good news of Jesus Christ.

As I grew more in the Lord and gave more of myself to him, I began to feel more passion for the lost souls. I did not want to just sit in a pew anymore. I wanted to go out and reach the lost sheep that I could see were hurt, in pain, anguished and needed someone to reach out to them. During this time of feeling the desire in me, God called me and my wife Alicia to pastor "The Second Evangelical Crusade" church.

At this point, my wife and I began to give out to the community as we saw the need that was so abundant around us. Between the brothers and sisters in the church we cooked food and freely gave to those in need. My wife and I were given donations upon donations of clothes and items in which we were able to give out every week to the community.

We knew that through this, God was pleased because he teaches us in his word to be selfless. I have learned that in order to be blessed, we need to be a blessing and this is part of ministering to the lost. Jesus said, "³⁵For I was hungry and you gave me something to eat, I was thirsty and you gave me something to drink, I was a stranger and you invited me in, [36] I needed clothes and you clothed me, I was sick and you looked after me, I was in prison and you came to visit me.' As we give we know that we are giving to the Lord. This was exciting to us because it gave us the opportunity to reach out to the lost and share the love of Jesus in which they were in dire need of. Not only did we reach out to the local community but we also were able to donate clothes and food items to Africa, Peru and Santo Domingo.

My wife and I had also been providing religious services and pastoral care at Buena Vida Continuing Care & Rehabilitation Center in Brooklyn, NY for over five years to the residents. We have devoted our time and services in order to meet the spiritual needs of the residents of Buena Vida. We have assisted the residents in coping with their losses, searching for meaning in life and helping them to adjust to living in a nursing home. It is a pleasure being able to do what Jesus would have done if he was still here walking on earth. But we are his hands and feet and we have been called to do the work he wants us to do for his glory.

While pastoring *The Second Evangelical Crusade*, I became a member of the 83rd Clergy Council, where I served as Assistant Treasurer. There I worked together with the police force to talk about how we can better serve the community. I was also a member of C.H.I.P.S. which stands for Chaplains Helping in Police Situations. There we served the community, outside the four-walls of the church. We did roll calls and provided spiritual counseling when needed or requested. We prayed for God's continuous protection over the police men and women who serve to protect our community.

I knew what it was to be cast down, rejected, sick and with no hope. This is why I am passionate about people who believe they have no hope, who are sick, who are in need, because I was there and I know that there is a solution and I have that solution that I can give to them for free and that is God's love.

Even David, the author of the Psalms, who was much loved of God, knew what it was to be cast down and dejected. He had tasted defeat in his life and felt the frustration of feeling hopeless and without strength in himself.

In Psalms 42:11 he cries out, "Why, my soul, are you downcast? Why so disturbed within me? Put your hope in God, for I will yet praise him, my Savior and my God."

Now there is an exact parallel to this in caring for the sheep. Only those intimately acquainted with sheep and their habits understand the significance of a cast sheep or a cast down sheep.

This is an old English shepherd's term for a sheep that has turned over on its back and cannot get up again by itself.

A cast sheep is a very sad thing to see. Lying on its back, its feet in the air, it flays away frantically, struggling to stand up, without success. Sometimes it will make a little sound or noise for help, but generally it lies there lashing about in frightened frustration.

If the owner does not arrive on the scene within a reasonably short time, the sheep will die.

This is but another reason why it is so essential for a sheep-man to look over his flock every day, counting them to see that all are able to be up and on their feet. If one or two are missing, often the first thought to flash into his mind is, one of my sheep is cast down somewhere. I must go in search of the lost sheep and set it on its feet again. Today people are cast down on so many things like depression, alcoholism, drugs, porn, adultery, sickness, fear, just to name a few. Just to let you know, if you are in a situation where you feel you are cast down, there is a way out and that way out is Jesus. He can restore you and bring you up to your feet once again.

I would like to mention that not only are we in search of the lost sheep physically, but we are also searching for them spiritually through prayer. It is impossible for us to be in two places at one time, but God can be all over the world at the same time. There is nothing impossible for God. Isa 43:13 says "from eternity to eternity I am God, no one can oppose what I do. No one can reverse my actions." Nothing is impossible when you put your trust, In God. Nothing is impossible when you're trusting in his word.

I thank God for my wife Alicia who is a prayer warrior. Each morning about 3 am she is on her knees praying for all the lost sheep that are suffering all over the world, and whatever the circumstance may be, they are out there, cast down, helpless, close to death, hurting and crying; and we know that God can reach out to them through our prayers.

Our prayers can get them out of the bad and sad condition that they are in. I thank God for a praying father who never gave up on me; and God answered his prayer because now I am free from alcohol addiction and I am walking in the truth of God's word. I had been that lost sheep hurting and drowning in addiction. But what God did for me, he can do for you. He set me free and he can set you free and your loved ones too.

Luke 15:7 states, "I tell you that in the same way there will be more rejoicing in heaven over one sinner who repents than over ninety-nine righteous persons who do not need to repent. The angels are waiting for you to repent my friend, so they can celebrate in heaven.

FOR THE SON OF MAN CAME TO SEEK AND SAVE THAT WHICH WAS LOST. LUKE 19:10

Examples of Sheep keepers in the Bible

Shepherds of the Old Testament

Genesis 4:2
Abel was a keeper of sheep.
"Later she gave birth to his brother Abel. Now Abel kept flocks, and Cain worked the soil."

Genesis 13:5
Lot was a keeper of sheep.
"⁵ Now Lot, who was moving about with Abram, also had flocks and herds and tents."

Genesis 29:9
Rachel was a keeper of sheep.
"⁹ While he was still talking with them, Rachel came with her father's sheep, for she was a shepherd."

Genesis 31:4

Jacob was a keeper of sheep.

"⁴ So Jacob sent word to Rachel and Leah to come out to the fields where his flocks were."

Genesis : 46:31-32

Joseph's brothers were keeper of sheep.

"³¹ Then Joseph said to his brothers and to his father's household, "I will go up and speak to Pharaoh and will say to him, 'My brothers and my father's household, who were living in the land of Canaan, have come to me. ³² The men are shepherds; they tend livestock, and they have brought along their flocks and herds and everything they own.'

Exodus 2:16

The daughters of Jethro, priest of Midian were keepers of sheep.

"¹⁶ Now a priest of Midian had seven daughters, and they came to draw water and fill the troughs to water their father's flock.

Exodus 3:1

Moses was a sheep keeper.

"Now Moses was tending the flock of Jethro his father-in-law, the priest of Midian, and he led the flock to the far side of the wilderness and came to Horeb, the mountain of God.

1 Samuel 16:11

David was a sheep keeper.

"So he asked Jesse, "Are these all the sons you have?"

"There is still the youngest," Jesse answered. "He is tending the sheep." Samuel said, "Send for him; we will not sit down until he arrives."

Shepherds of the New Testament
(Jesus the Great Shepherd)

Luke 2:8
"And there were shepherds living out in the fields nearby, keeping watch over their flocks at night."

Mark 14:27
"You will all fall away," Jesus told them, "for it is written: 'I will strike the shepherd, and the sheep will be scattered.'

1 Peter2:25
For "you were like sheep going astray," but now you have returned to the Shepherd and Overseer of your souls."

John 10:16
"I have other sheep that are not of this sheep pen. I must bring them also. They too will listen to my voice, and there shall be one flock and one shepherd."

Hebrews 13:20
"Now may the God of peace, who through the blood of the eternal covenant brought back from the dead our Lord Jesus, that great Shepherd of the sheep."

1 Peter 5:4
"And when the Chief Shepherd appears, you will receive the crown of glory that will never fade away."

"In Search of the Lost Sheep Ministries" has always believed and will continue to believe in giving to the community by feeding the homeless, clothing the naked, visiting the sick and giving a word of encouragement through prayer and spiritual guidance.

Giving to the Community

Here are some of the items and products given to the ministry by <u>Here's Life Inner City</u> which in turn were given out for free to the community.

Free clothes available for those in the community.

Pastor Cortes picking up boxes of canned goods to give out to the community.

Community Outreach.

Pastor Alicia Cortes helps to pack up boxes of canned goods.

Pastor Calet Cortes taking bread to provide for others.

Isaiah 58:10

[10] *If* you extend your soul to the hungry
And satisfy the afflicted soul,
Then your light shall dawn in the darkness,
And your darkness shall be as the noonday

Missions trip to Santo Domingo/Dominican Republic: 2011

Celebrating with the children of the community after talking to them about Jesus and handing out free toys and candy.

Pastor Alicia Cortes gives a toy to a little child.

Pastor Alicia and members of the community singing songs of thanksgiving.

Pastor Calet Cortes Jr. and Pastor Javier Dextre.

Pastors Calet and Alicia Cortes doing community work in the state of Florida.

Visiting the sick is something that Jesus taught.

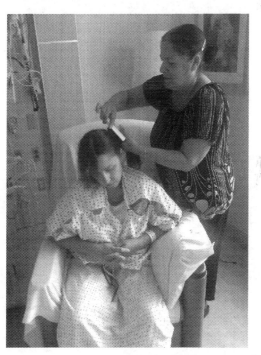

A true joy to encourage and pray for those in need.

Det. Dennis Diaz from the 83rd Precinct, Community Affairs along with Pastor Calet Cortes Jr. on the National Night Out Against Crime.

Pastors Calet and Alicia Cortes taking time to do volunteer work at the nursing home.

Association of Hispanic Ministers

"Clamor por Nueva York," President Obispo Dr. Luis Paniagua, Pastors, Chaplains, including former Mayor Michael Bloomberg from the City of New York.

The Second Evangelical Crusade Church.

Matthew 25:34-36,

[34] Then the King will say to those on His right hand, 'Come, you blessed of My Father, inherit the kingdom prepared for you from the foundation of the world: [35] for I was *hungry* and you gave Me food; I was *thirsty* and you gave Me drink; I was a *stranger* and you took Me in; [36] I *was **naked*** and you clothed Me; I was *sick* and you visited Me; I was in ***prison*** and you came to Me.' [40] And the King will answer and say to them, 'Assuredly, I say to you, inasmuch as you did *it* to one of the least of these My brethren, you did *it* to ***Me.***'

In Search of the Lost Sheep Ministry
2114 Walden Park Circle, #103
Kissimmee, FL 34744

Beloved,

I would like to take the opportunity to personally thank you for your presence at the memorial service for the wonderful man of God, Calet Cortes, Sr. Thank you also for the prayers and support you've extended to the family during this difficult time. May God Bless you greatly!

With Much Love,
Rev. Calet & Alicia Cortes

Calet Cortes, Sr.
1927-2014

PRAYER

If you want to accept the Lord Jesus Christ into your heart
just simply say this prayer;

Father, I give my heart to you today. I know I am not perfect but I know you are. I know that in my weakness you are strong. I ask that you forgive me and erase my sins as far as the East is from the West. I surrender my life to you. I give you my insecurities, my depression, my sickness, my pain, my sorrows, all to you. Please make me pleasing in your sight and find favor upon me. Lord Jesus, keep me safe in your arms and always send your angels to encamp around me day and night. I pray you will give me the strength to follow you all the days of my life. In Jesus' name I pray, Amen.

ABOUT THE AUTHORS

Calet Cortes Jr. is the founder and president of "In Search of the Lost Sheep Ministries." He has served as a member of the Hispanic Pentecostal church "La Cruzada Evangelica," pastored by Reverend Nelson Aponte and he himself was Pastor of "The Second Evangelical Crusade" church" in Brooklyn, New York. While residing in New York, Calet became very involved in the community, reaching out to everyone he knew was in need. Having the desire to do more to serve the community Calet joined an organization called C.H.I.P.S. (Chaplains Helping in Police Situations) in October of 2003. He also served as a member in the 83rd precinct clergy council in February of 2004. In addition, Calet also was a member of the 90th Precinct clergy in January of 2007. Calet Cortes was ordained as Pastor in July 2004. Not only did he serve the community with vigilance but he also served with contributions and donations of goods, clothes and even continued this mission into the missionary field in which he had the opportunity to go to Puerto Rico, Dominican Republic, Mexico and Spain. Now residing in Kissimmee, Florida; Calet continues to spread the love of Jesus to all through donations of goods and open generosity but above all, letting people know that Jesus loves them and that He is coming back for those who have heard this message and have accepted the Lord as their personal Savior.

Marisol Bennett is the daughter of Calet Cortes Jr. She was born and raised in a Christian home by the guidance of her parents who not only preached the gospel but lived it according to what the scriptures say in Proverbs 22:6 to [6] "Train up a child in the way he should go, And when he is old he will not depart from it." Marisol has been involved in the ministry while growing up in church. She volunteered in Children's Church. She was involved in the plays and dramas that her father produced. She was even a part of the puppet ministry in which her father and her sister Elizabeth along with Elizabeth's daughter Lillian Torres arranged in order to reach the lost sheep and bring them to Christ through a little comedy but legitimacy that always involved an altar call. Growing up, Marisol began to play the guitar and sing in the church. She loves the Lord and works hard to make sure that her children are also being taught to walk in the right path as Proverbs 22:6 says to [6] "Train up a child in the way he should go, And when he is old he will not depart from it." Marisol is a great supporter of "In Search of the Lost Sheep Ministries" and will continue the journey of bringing light into this dark world.

INDEX

King James Version (KJV)

To contact the Authors, Please write to:

In Search of the Lost Sheep Ministries
Pastor Calet Cortes Jr.
2114 Walden Park Circle Apt 103
Kissimmee, Fl 34744

Website: WWW.INSEARCHOFTHELOSTSHEEP.COM
Email: Insearchofthelostsheep@yahoo.com
Phone: (407) 910-4905
Fax: (407) 910-4905

To make a financial contribution to this ministry, go to:
www.insearchofthelostsheep.com
and click on donation.

ABOUT US

In Search of the Lost Sheep is a Christian Community Outreach Ministry headed by Rev. Calet Cortes, with the help and support of his wife, Alicia Cortes, out of Kissimmee, Florida. The Ministry strives to be the hands and feet of Jesus by providing for the immediate needs of the community, all the while promoting the way, truth, and the life, through the message of salvation through Christ.

The ministry has been in operation for approximately 25 years. Rev. Calet Cortes first began the Ministry in Brooklyn, NY. Since its start all those years ago, the Ministry has been able to impact people all across the country and around the world, ministering to people across the 5 boroughs of NYC, across various cities in Florida, and even to numerous towns in Puerto Rico. Rev. Cortes has vowed to continue to do the work of the Lord as long as he has breath in him!

NOTES

Printed in the United States
By Bookmasters